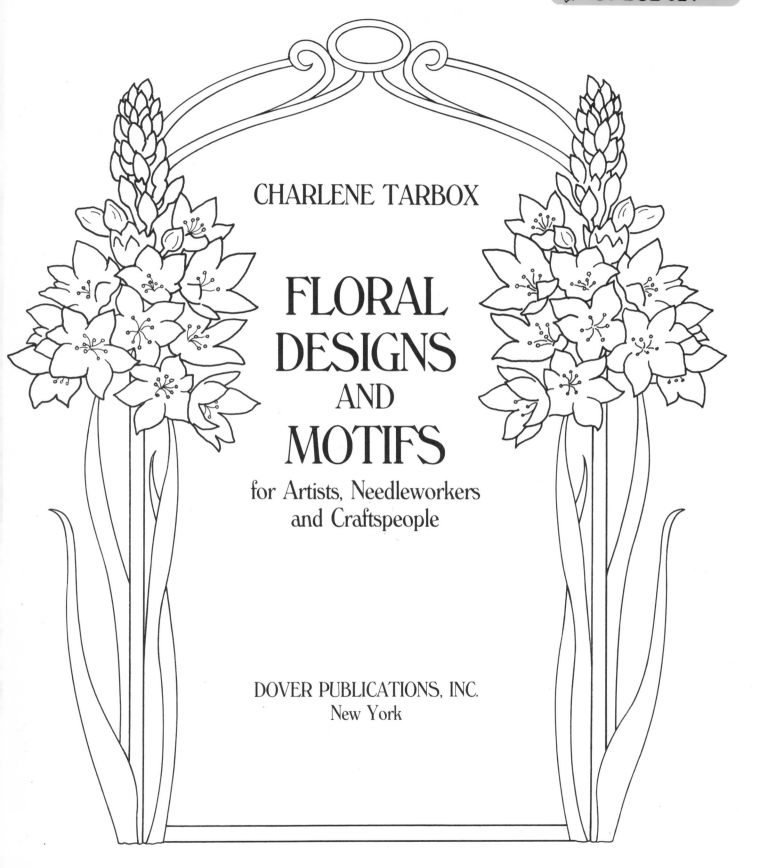

CHARLENE TARBOX

FLORAL DESIGNS AND MOTIFS

for Artists, Needleworkers
and Craftspeople

DOVER PUBLICATIONS, INC.
New York

*To Oliver, for his
patience and encouragement*

———— • ————

Title page illustration:
Chincherinchee (Wonder Flower)
Copyright page illustration:
Shooting Star
Alphabetical List page illustration:
Virginia Bluebell

———— • ————

Published in Canada by General Publishing Company, Ltd., 30 Lesmill Road, Don Mills, Toronto, Ontario.

Published in the United Kingdom by Constable and Company, Ltd.

Floral Designs and Motifs for Artists, Needleworkers and Craftspeople is a new work, first published by Dover Publications, Inc., in 1984.

DOVER *Pictorial Archive* SERIES

Manufactured in the United States of America
Dover Publications, Inc., 31 East 2nd Street, Mineola, N.Y. 11501

Library of Congress Cataloging-in-Publication Data

Tarbox, Charlene.
Floral designs and motifs for artists, needleworkers, and craftspeople.

(Dover pictorial archive series)
1. Decoration and ornament—Plant forms—Themes, motives. I. Title. II. Series.
NK1560.T37   1984   745.4   84-7969
ISBN 0-486-24716-3 (pbk.)

PUBLISHER'S NOTE

Of all the motifs that have been used in decorative art through the ages and in every culture, florals are probably the most beloved. To provide artists, needleworkers and craftspeople with exactly the kind of attractive line renderings of flowers they need, Charlene Tarbox, a New York City painter, illustrator, fabric designer and teacher, has created the nearly 140 original designs in this book. Her interpretations of the infinitely varied forms of flowering plants show great sensitivity and mastery of pen-and-ink technique.

Each flower or plant illustrated in this collection is identified by its common name. In some cases, the names given are quite specific (Large Yellow Pond Lily, Bird's-foot Violet); in other cases, they are more or less generic (the Orchids, only three of which—the Lady's Slipper, Helleborine and Rosebud Orchid—have specific designations). No attempt has been made to provide systematic technical nomenclature.

In instances where a plant is equally well known by a common name of English origin and another vernacular name that is the same as its botanical name (e.g., Coreopsis or Tickseed), both names are given in the captions and in the Alphabetical List of Flowers Illustrated overleaf. (In the case of the Geraniums, it should be noted that the cultivated form shown on page 6 and its wild relative on page 7 are quite different from the plant that generally goes by that name, the florist's Geranium, which is technically *Pelargonium*. All belong to the same family.)*

Ms. Tarbox has chosen a wide variety of plants as subjects for her designs. Cultivated garden flowers are the best represented, and they span the seasons from the Crocus of early spring to the autumnal Chrysanthemum. Such popular types as Roses and Tulips are shown in a number of horticultural varieties, and in several decorative treatments. A few favorite houseplants figure in as well: African Violet and Gloxinia.

Certain of the plants that thrive unwanted in our lawns and flowerbeds have delightful blossoms in spite of their weediness, and a few of these are included here: the Bindweeds, Chicory (which is also cultivated in several forms) and Butter-and-eggs or Toadflax. Those who spurn these "weeds" should recall that a rosebush is a weed if it grows in a cornfield. Look closely at these blooms and you will see their kinship to showier domesticated species: the Bindweeds are relatives of Morning Glories, and Butter-and-eggs is cousin to the Snapdragon.

Native wildflowers of woodland and field are not neglected in this volume. Most of those included here are typical of the northeastern United States and neighboring Canada, but the West is represented by the Redwood Sorrel and the Wild Lupine.

For their popularity as design motifs and general appeal, Ms. Tarbox has included a number of drawings of plants not usually thought of for their flowers: Holly, Oak, Pine, Maple, Grape, Strawberry (wild and tame), Raspberry, Hazelnut and Mistletoe. There are also some pictures of trees and shrubs that are grown primarily for their blossoms: Dogwood, Leatherleaf and Bog Rosemary.

Ms. Tarbox demonstrates a versatility of execution which users of this Pictorial Archive material will appreciate. Some of her drawings are very naturalistic and others are quite stylized. She has captured the essential forms without fussy technical detail, and needleworkers especially will be grateful for her discrimination and fine sense of design. Decorative applications are the focus, and many of the designs will work well as borders, frames, corner cuts, and other frequently needed devices. The clarity of line will make reproduction, enlargement or reduction trouble-free, and of course all the art (up to ten designs in any single project or publication) may be used without special permission.

---

*Those interested in the fascinating, if sometimes confusing subject of plant nomenclature will enjoy *How Plants Get Their Names* by Liberty Hyde Bailey (Dover, 1963, 20796-X).

ALPHABETICAL LIST OF FLOWERS ILLUSTRATED

Narcissus   Thunbergia   5

6   Geranium   Gaillardia

Rose

Wild Geranium

Impatiens

Frostweed

Bindweed

Rose

Hibiscus

Gaillardia

Day Lily   Blackberry Lily

Columbine

Jack-in-the-pulpit

Holly

13

Tickseed (Coreopsis)

Periwinkle   Morning Glory

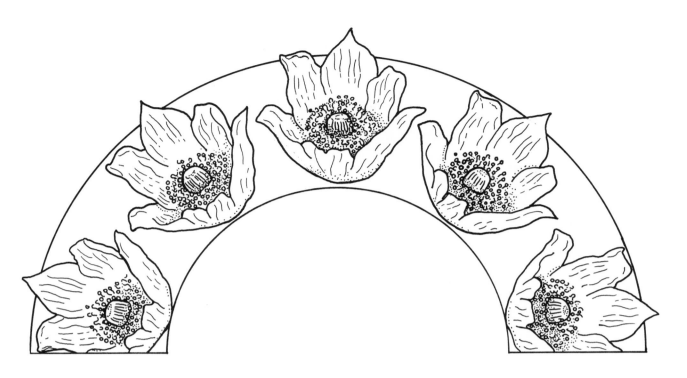

Pasqueflower

Low Bindweed

Wild Strawberry

Poppy

Lily

Cosmos

Tulip

Gloxinia

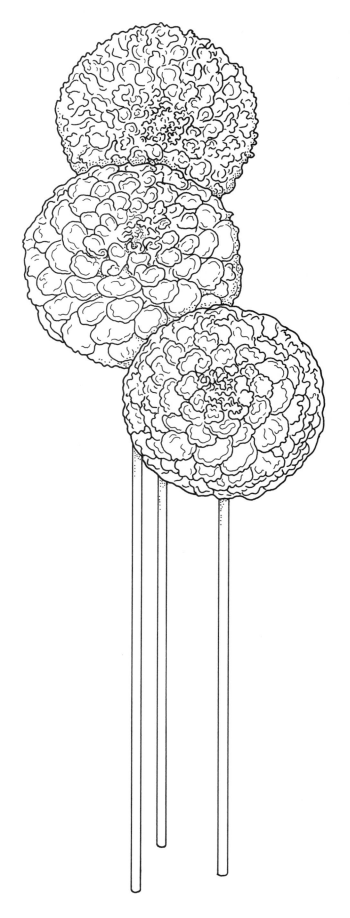

Harebell   Dahlia

Rose

Oak

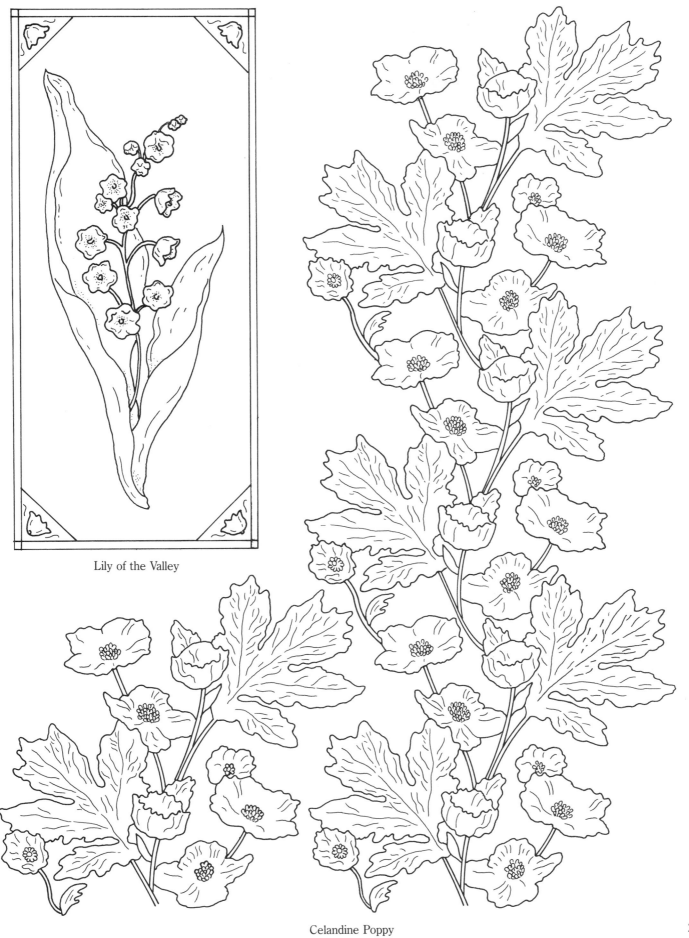

Lily of the Valley

Celandine Poppy

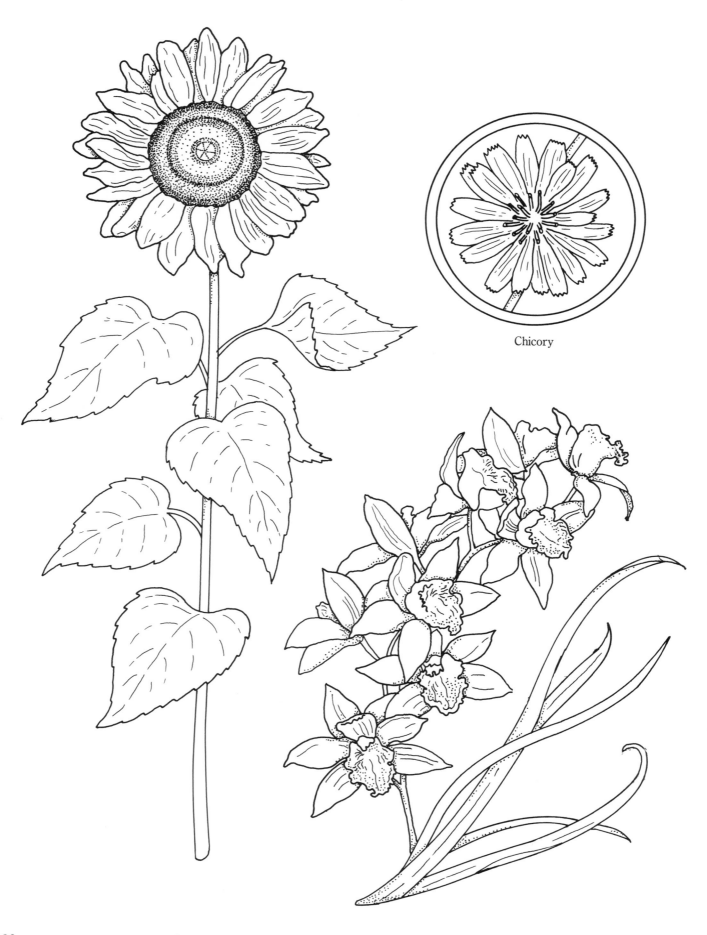

Chicory

Sunflower   Orchid

Kerria (Japanese Rose)

Pansy   Bog Rosemary

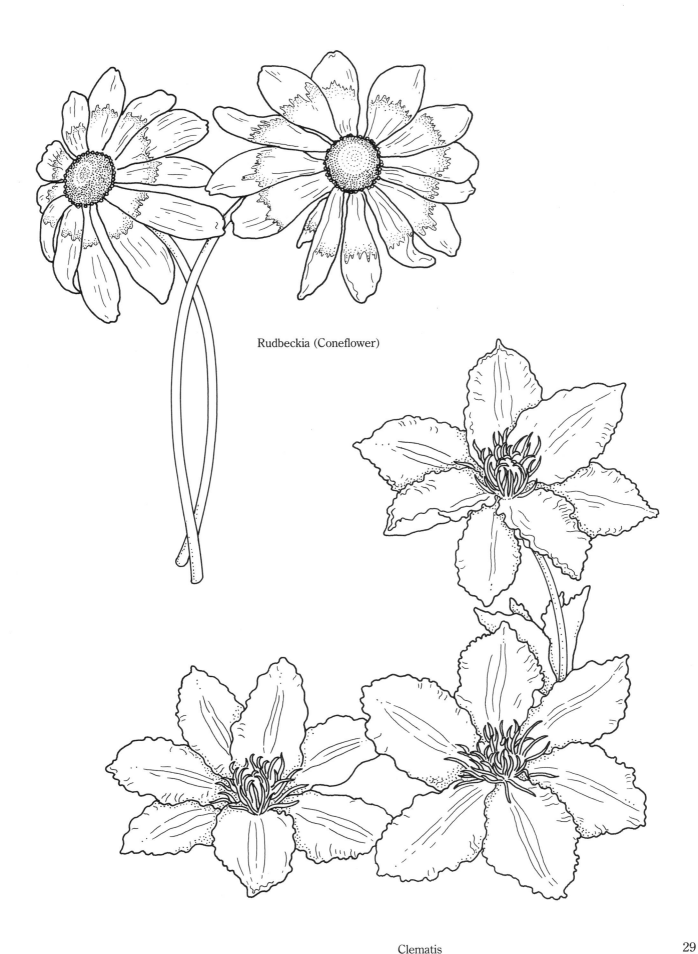

Rudbeckia (Coneflower)

Clematis

Day Lily

Zinnia

Bellflower

Orchid

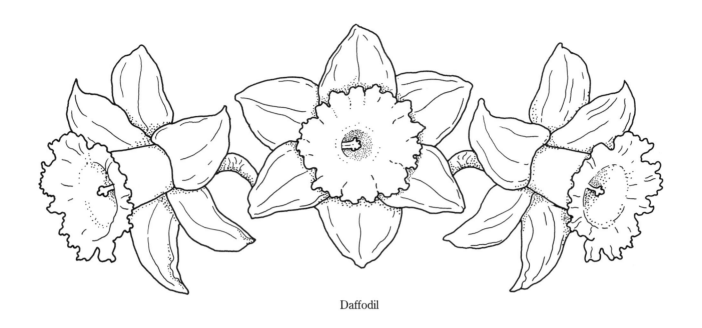

Daffodil

Rose

Leatherleaf

Orchid   Chocolate Lily

Sacred Lotus   Freesia

Camellia

African Violet

Gladiolus

Double Begonia

Magnolia   Evening Primrose

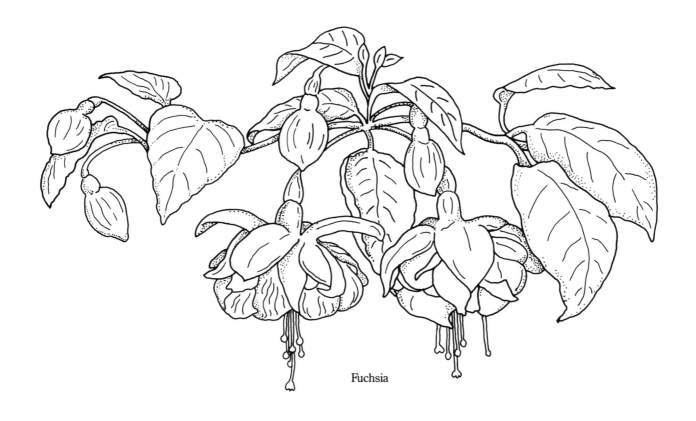

Fuchsia

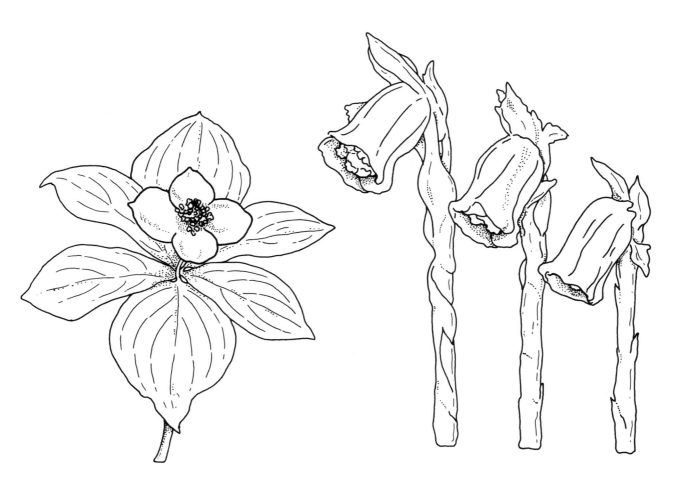

Bunchberry

Indian Pipe

Rosebud Orchid   Narcissus

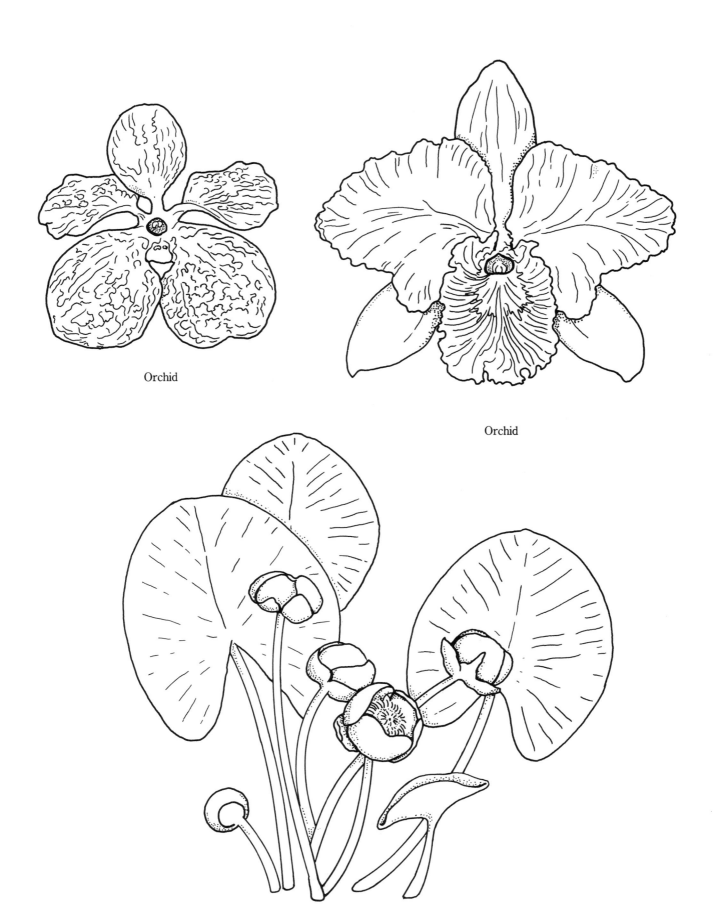

Orchid

Orchid

Large Yellow Pond Lily

39

Globeflower

Scabiosa

Double Tulip

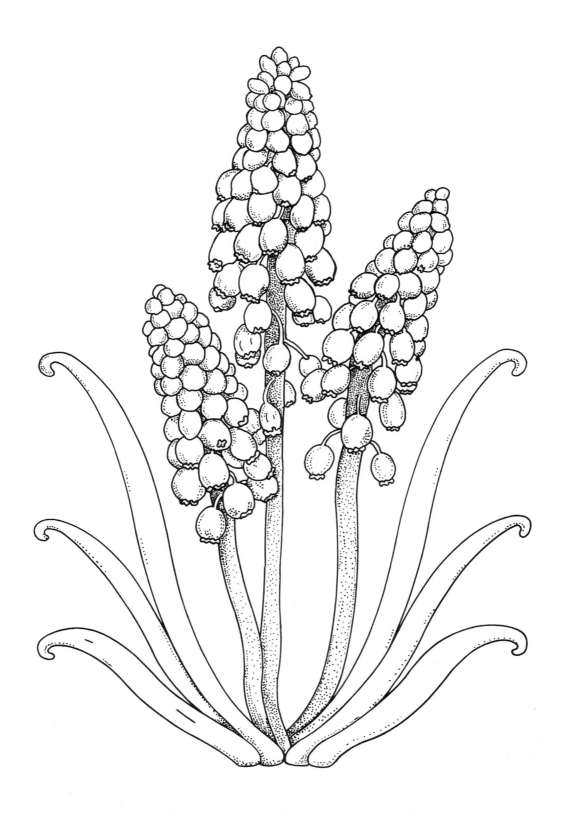

Grape Hyacinth

Sweet Pea

Trillium

Rose

Rose

Lady's Slipper

Parrot Tulip

Tulip

Orchid   Gentian

Maple   Common Blue Violet   49

Oxeye Daisy

Oxeye Daisy

Purple Gerardia

Water Lily

52   Closed Gentian   Forget-me-not

Grape

Pine

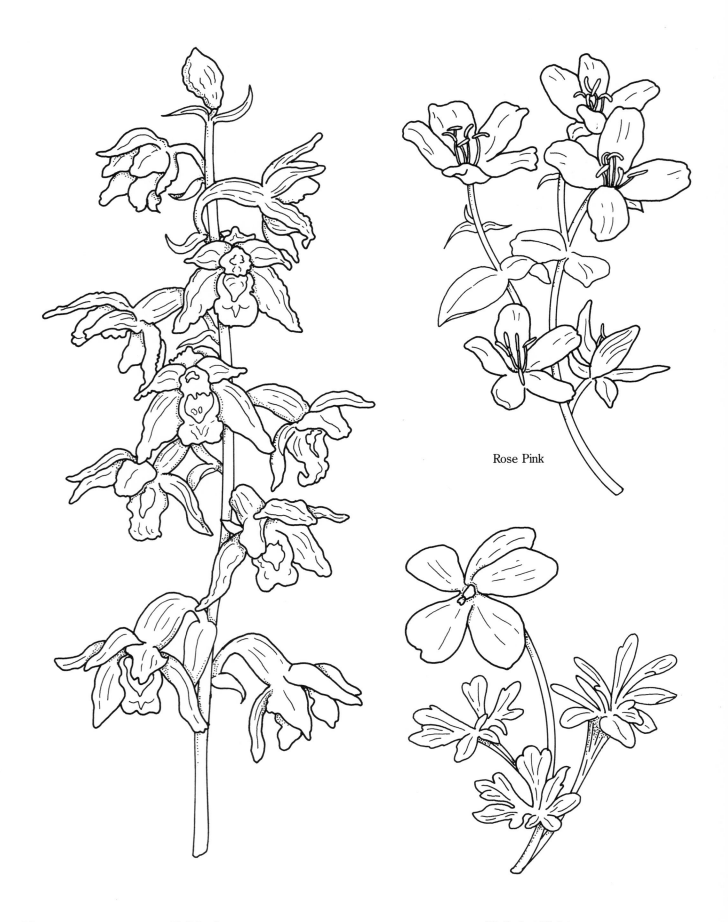

Rose Pink

54   Helleborine   Bird's-foot Violet

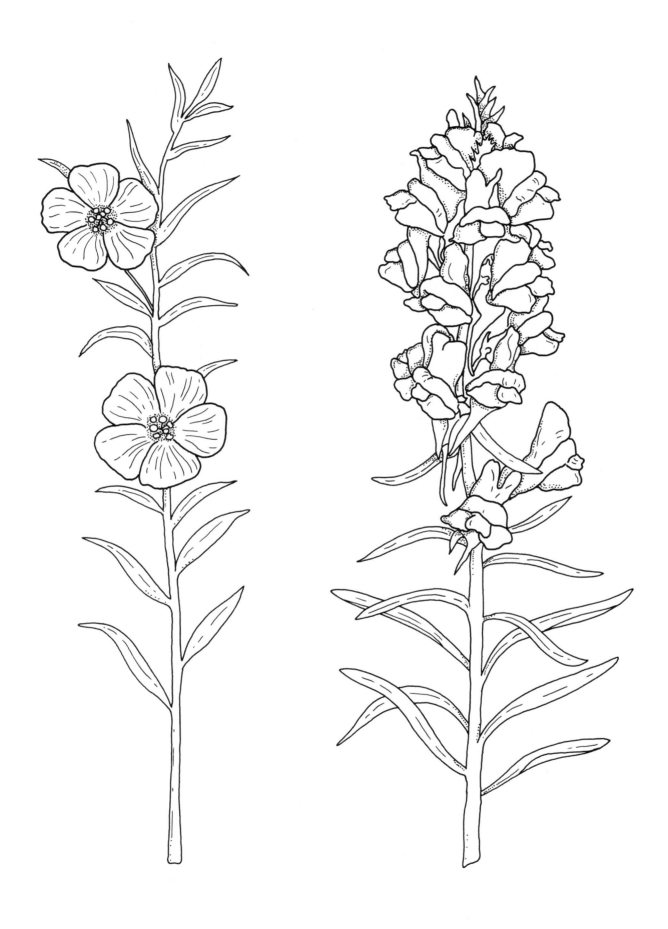

Flax   Butter-and-eggs (Toadflax)   55

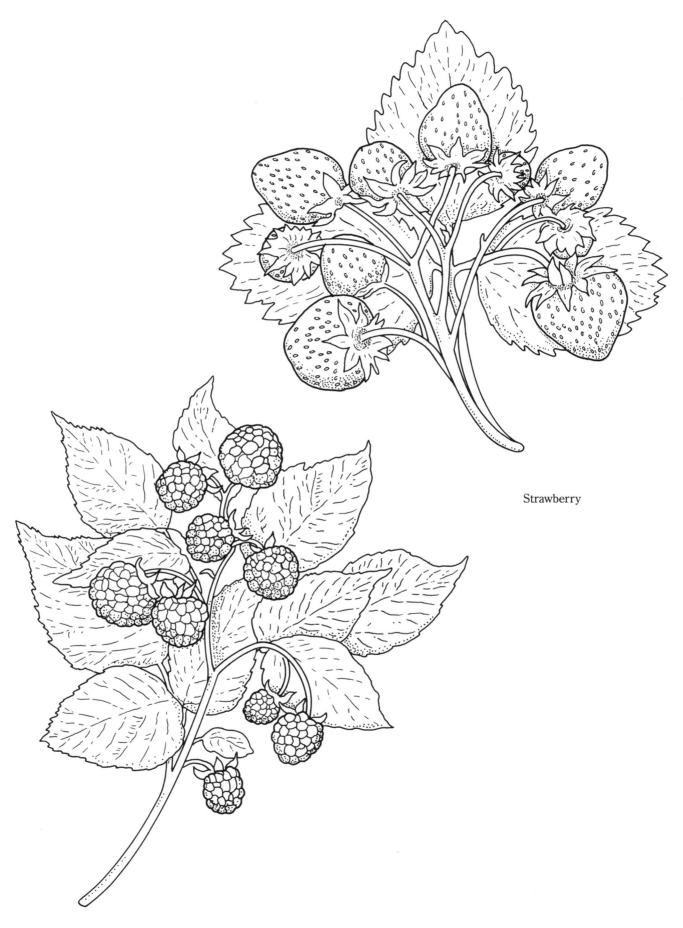

Strawberry

Raspberry

Sunflower

Wild Calla

Poppy

Marigold

Chrysanthemum

Redwood Sorrel with Grasses

Dogwood

Mistletoe

Primula

Holly

Bellflower

Dogwood

Willow Herb

Aster

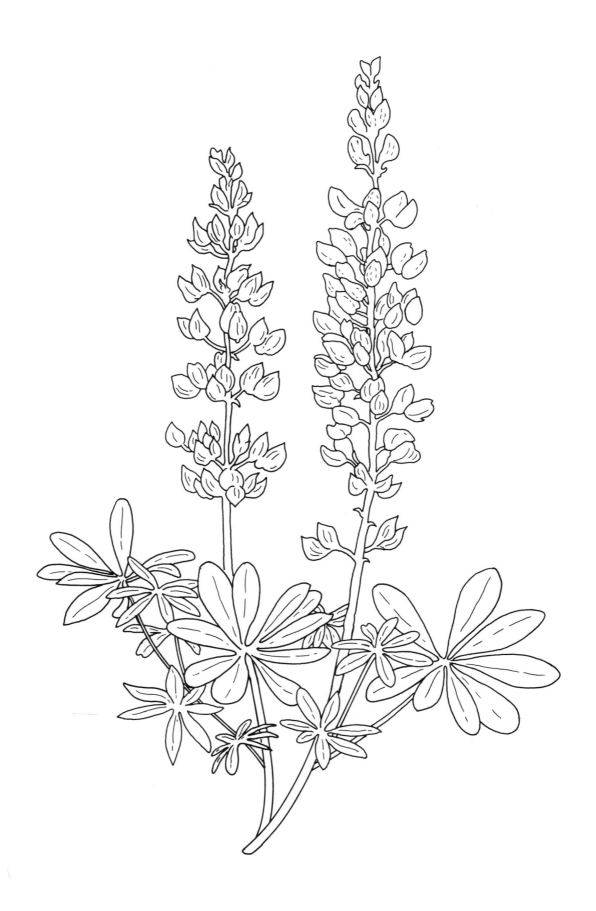

Wild Lupine

Dahlia

Wild Iris

Carnation

Tiger Lily

Oxalis

Dahlia

Crocus

Leatherflower   Chrysanthemum

Anemone

Anemone

Protea

Protea

75

Hazelnut (Filbert)

Daffodil

Monkey Flower

Scilla   Marshmallow

Aztec Lily

Fire Pink